WORLDS L

WORLDS ENOUGH

Poems for and about Children

(*and a few grown-ups*)

by

Scott Owens

Illustrated by

Missy Cleveland

REDHAWK PUBLICATIONS

Copyright ©2022, Text, Scott Owens; Illustrations, Missy Cleveland

All rights reserved. This book or parts thereof may not be reproduced in any form, stored in any retrieval system, or transmitted in any form by any means—electronic, mechanical, photocopy, recording, or otherwise—without prior written permission of the publisher, except as provided by United States of America copyright law. For permission requests, write to the publisher, at "Attention: Permissions Coordinator," at the address below.

Redhawk Publications
The Catawba Valley Community College Press
2550 US Hwy 70 SE
Hickory NC 28602

ISBN: 978-1-952485-73-2
Library of Congress Number: 2022937216

FOR

Damian	Casey
Keegan	Bradley
Sawyer	Logan
Tanner	Izak
Quinn	Hasan
Selby	Olivia
Beau	Arwen
Camryn	Aylan
Connor	Anna
Maggie	Jonathan
Will	Ferah
Rosie	Emma
Jessica	Kate
Christian	Timothy
Katie	Michael
Evie	Mattie
Jacob	David
Amanda	Thomas
Trevor	Legacy
Sam	Margaret
Madison	Marie
Caleb	Macen
Harper	Callum
Kirsten	Parker

And every other child we might have inspired
while they were inspiring us.

This project is supported by a grant from the United Arts Council of Catawba County.

Thank you, UACCC!

WORLDS ENOUGH

CURIOUS ABOUT THE SKY

Sawyer Makes the Sky at 2	13
What Beau Knows	14
Scary Story	16
Playground	18
Words of Warning	19
Stay Wild	20
Maggie's Magnificent Memory	22
Timothy, Thomathy, and Finn	23
My School Is a Zoo	24
Things to Do with a Leaf Pile	27
Recycler	29
Too Many Pets	30
Sawyer's Underwater Wonders	33
Faces	34
A Penny Saved	36
How to Get Rid of the Hiccups	37
Alliterative Abecedarian	38
School Time	41
On Botany and Eminem	43
Dear Humpty Dumpty	44
How to Enjoy a Spring Day	45
Night Travel	47
I'm Thankful for the Week after Next	48

RIDDLE ME THIS

Circles	50
Ben's Friend	52
A Bit of Nothing	53
I Bet I Can Make You Cry	54
Essential	56
A Most Unusual Room	57
How to Use U's	59
Besties	61
Storm Warning	62
Clapperer	63

A FEW HAIKU

By the Numbers	66
[I am going to]	67
[fashion's free thinker]	68
[knee high grass]	69
[picking blackberries]	70
[to plant a rose bush]	71
[one]	72
[backyard lightning bugs]	73
[the moon not quite full]	74
[honeysuckle smell]	75
[imagine]	76
[the origami]	77

WORLDS ENOUGH UNFOLDING

Sky of Endless Stars	81
Sawyer Says	82
I Teach My Daughter the Joy of Sound	85
Here Lies	87
The Word for What Only 4-Year Olds Can See	88
Sawyer at 7 Discovers the Roundness of the World	89
Flavors	90
Headstrong Terry	91
Words and What They Say	92
Of	93
Assurances	95
Onomatopoeia 101	96
About the Author	99
About the Artist	101

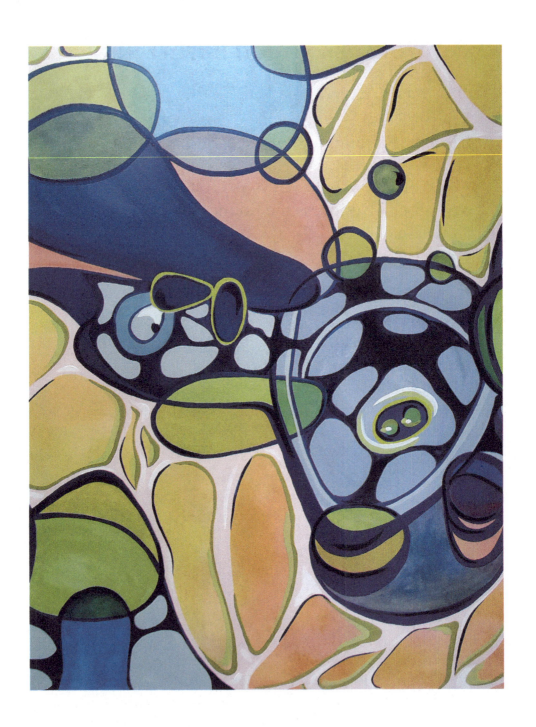

CURIOUS ABOUT THE SKY

Worlds Enough

Sawyer Makes the Sky at 2

She puts it together like anything
you might imagine, stroke by stroke
spreading blue across the page
and beyond the page, pencil-thin
brushes extending the world of possibility
beyond any arbitrary border of paper,
mat, table, but saving always
enough room for one red ball of sun.

What Beau Knows

Even at 4, there's so much that Beau knows
and so much more he'll learn as he grows.
Beau knows how to hug a bear,
choose a pair of antlers to wear,
ride the rides they have at the fair,
how to catch a fish or a salamander,
make something grand that much grander.
Beau knows how to dunk his head in a mountain creek,
climb a mountain to its tiptop peak,
keep real quiet when he's trying to sneak.
He knows how to beat his mom at Uno,
craft some newfangled gizmo,
paint a seahorse or a mermaid,
pull up a corner to show off a band-aid,
how to give excellent butterfly kisses,
and listen intently when Mimi reminisces.
Beau knows about Eskimos and buffalos,
puppet shows and radios,
little brothers and robots and trucks,
feeding giraffes and butterflies and ducks.

Poems for and about Children

Beau knows how to dig a deep hole
and make a swing go,
how to roll down a hill,
and sled in the snow,
how to ride a bike or a rhino,
how to turn his tongue blue,
and avoid the beak of an emu.
And at the end of a long, long day
of running and laughter and play,
of learning what he needs to know,
Beau knows how tell a story,
or listen to one being told,
and the way he snuggles reveals
Beau knows how great it feels
to just lie down and rest.

Scary Story

Playing hide and seek once
I hid beneath a chair
and although I didn't mean to
I gave them quite a scare.

The chair was brown
and low to the ground
with a skirt that went
all the way around.

There was hardly any space
concealed beneath the chair
so no one else had ever thought
of hiding themselves there.

But I was small
and could squeeze in tight
so beneath it I did crawl
and hid out of the light.

They looked and looked
but couldn't find me
till at last they called out
Olly, olly, oxen free!

Everyone came
from their hiding place
except for me.
I stayed in my space.

And not because
I didn't want to be near them,
but just because
I couldn't really hear them.

They searched the whole house.
They searched underneath.
They called the neighbors.
They called the police.

They looked all down the street
and through the back alley
without me even knowing
the game had reached its finale.

For hours I stayed there
and made not a peep,
not because I was good
but because I was asleep.

At last, around dark
when my nap was done,
I pulled myself out
and asked if I'd won.

Playground

I have a cave beneath the scuppernong,
my favorite place to go.
I enter it by lifting vines
and bending way down low.

It's not so hot beneath the limbs
and everything is green.
I play and play for hours
and keep myself unseen.

It's bigger than you might expect
and the smell is awfully sweet
and if I get hungry while I play
there are all these grapes to eat.

Whenever I want to be alone
I crawl beneath the scuppernong
but I think that I might like it better
if you'd agree to come along.

Words of Warning

Summer day.
And I run outside to play.
Mama says, "Shut that door. You're letting out my air."
Papa says, "It's hot out. You best beware."

Wide open yard.
I take off running.
Mama says, "Oh, don't kick up so much dirt."
Papa says, "Just be careful you don't get hurt."

Fat blackberries
grow by the fence.
Mama says, "Make sure you don't eat too much."
Papa says, "Watch out for snakes and such."

Swing hanging from limb.
I pump my legs to make it go.
Mama says, "Don't twist like that. Make it go right."
Papa says, "You better just hold on tight."

Big old tree
begging to be climbed.
Mama says, "Careful you don't fall to the ground."
Papa says, "Whatever you do, just don't look down."

Darkening path
heads into woods.
Mama says, "Don't you go too far."
Papa says, "Just make sure we know where you are."

Tired at last
I come inside.
Mama says, "Go scrub those hands real good."
Papa says, "Dirt's just part of childhood."

Stay Wild
for Maurice

I'm going out, he says,
to anyone who isn't listening,
off the porch and through the yard,
out the gate that we keep barred,
past the topsy-turvy hens
pecking, prancing, dancing again,
flaunting highfalutin' feathers,
cackling loud and all together
just to get fluffed up enough,
past the pasture crowd of cattleproud
lowing deep and lowing gruff,
and flaying flies with fraying tails,
past the pond whose boat we rowed
and caught the wind in its little sails
to find the croaking toad's abode,
past the fence so long and frightening,
seeming like it's ever tightening.
I'm going out to the wildwoods
where the wild things are,
where dragons and giants come out to play
and chase my restlessness away,
where flowers bloom from every field
and cities rise from every hill,
where skies are blue and blowing wild
and welcome every dreaming child,
where everything that I can see
makes me think more endlessly.
But don't you worry. I won't go far,
just far enough to be farther away
than I could imagine yesterday.

Maggie's Magnificent Memory

Maggie remembered most everything.
She never forgot anything she learned,
how to dance, how to sing,
how to cook without getting burned.

She knew the names of each state,
each flower and rock,
how to draw every shape,
and how to read a clock.

She could recite poems whole
or make up her own rhymes,
perform any role,
and count pennies, nickels, and dimes.

Of course she knew her address
and addition, multiplication, and subtraction,
but what she knew best
was how to work without distraction.

She knew which bugs would sting
and the months from January to December.
Maggie remembered most everything
except what she forgot to remember.

Timothy, Thomathy, and Finn

Timothy, Thomathy, and Finn
always wanted to go out when they were in.

They would run and shout,
and throw things about.

They would find a ball they could kick
or build things with sticks.

They would swing from trees
and get mud on their knees.

They would hunt crickets and frogs
under rocks and logs,

and dig up earthworms
to make the girls squirm.

But mostly they liked to pretend
they were raptors who were trying to get in.

My School Is a Zoo

I've come to the conclusion
that my school is a zoo.
When you hear of who lives here
you'll think so too.

There's Samuel Lox
who's as smart as a fox,
Robert House
as quiet as a mouse.

There's Penelope Jewel
as stubborn as a mule,
and Timothy Figg
who eats like a pig.

There's my friend Sarafina
who laughs like a hyena
and Gabriel Toth
who's as slow as a sloth.

There's little Priscilla
as cute as a chinchilla
and then there's Jake
as mean as a snake.

And don't forget the teacher
who is somewhat a creature
because old Mrs. Faulk
watches us like a hawk.

Then, of course, there's me
as much an animal as any you've met
because, you see,
I'm the teacher's pet.

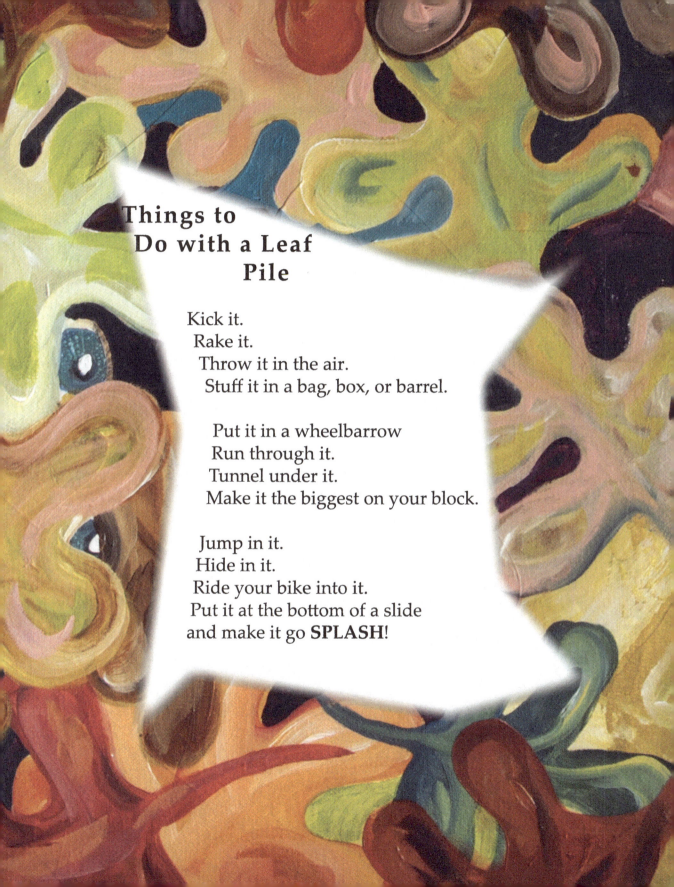

Things to Do with a Leaf Pile

Kick it.
Rake it.
Throw it in the air.
Stuff it in a bag, box, or barrel.

Put it in a wheelbarrow
Run through it.
Tunnel under it.
Make it the biggest on your block.

Jump in it.
Hide in it.
Ride your bike into it.
Put it at the bottom of a slide
and make it go **SPLASH**!

Recycler

I thank you God for most the amazing earthworm
For even though they may wriggle and squirm
Even though they seem slimy and wet
And no one ever wants them as a pet
Still they help fulfill all our wishes
By serving as bait for catching fishes
And it's really quite neat that they breathe through their skin
And if you cut them in half they'll grow back again
But by far the earthworms' most valuable trick
Is how they make our gardens fertile and rich.
Some call them rainworms, dew worms or night crawlers,
But their biggest job is to be a dirt overhauler.

Too Many Pets

My mother says I have too many pets
but I don't really see why she frets.
I have Huck and Finn, my two dogs,
and my rose-hair tarantula, Aragog.
My four cats are Nancy and Pip,
Neko (Japanese for cat) and Cool Whip.
Raja is the name of my tiger-morph gecko,
and the other is Igneous, whom I call Neo.
Four of my chickens are cochin bantams:
Spirit, Specter, Ghost, and Phantom.
And then I have four that are speckled Sussex:
Lance, Widow, Brigand, and my rooster, Duchess.
My tetras have names from *The Hunger Games*:
Finnick, Haymitch, Enobaria, and Seneca Crane.
My frogs are simply Zippy and Zoomer.
And my platys are Gimli, Legolas, and Boomer.
My swordtails are named after *Hobbit* good guys:
Frodo, Merry, Pippen, and Samwise.
My algae eater is Smeagle, and Gandalf's my loach.
My catfish are Crabbe, Goyle, and Draco.
My guppies will make my list nearly done:
there's Aragorn, Boromir and Jack Skellington.
Just one more set before I'm through.
My angels are Primrose, Katniss, and Rue.
I've listed each one here by name,
and doing so makes something quite plain.
No matter what I count, there's no more than four,
which says to me there's room for one more.

Sawyer's Underwater Wonders

When Sawyer goes under she sees
swimming 'round beneath the seas
such wonders that could only exist
at the bottom of a special abyss:
catfish with whiskers and tails,
octopi bigger than whales,
frogs blowing bubbles from pipes,
a seahorse with pink zebra stripes
seacows in snorkels and masks,
paddling from task to task,
and pigs in scuba gear
searching for a souvenir.

We'll never know how much of it's real
because on the surface we've stayed
knowing we're much too afraid
of the giant electric eel.

Faces

Everybody has a face
to wear when they go anyplace.
In fact, we all have more than one.
Some are serious, and some are fun.
Some are angry, and some are sad.
Some are worried, and some are glad.
Some are clever, and some are weepy.
Some are lively, and some are sleepy.
Some are frowning, and some are watching.
Some are laughing, and some are shocking.
Faces tell you how I feel.
None are fake. They all are real.
All these faces that are part of me
help me be how I need to be.

A Penny Saved

I have a penny in my shoe.
I don't know how it got there
or what good it will do.
A penny's not enough to share,

and you can't buy much with a penny today.
Maybe I should just throw it away.
I could toss it into a wishing well
and hope it brings me something swell.

I could flip it up into the air
to see if it lands on heads or tails
but then it might roll anywhere
if my attempt to catch it fails.

I could take it out and spin it
or have a drawing for someone to win it.
I could flatten it on a railroad track,
but then I might not get it back.

I have a penny in my shoe
Maybe I should give it to you.
But I doubt that you would really care,
so I think that I'll just leave it there.

How to Get Rid of the Hiccups

While drinking water, use a straw
and surely the hiccups will withdraw.

If not, take a deep breath, count to ten;
hopefully the hiccups will be gone by then.

Or get a paper bag and put it in place
completely over your hiccupping face.

If those solutions prove to be a sham,
have them scared from your diaphragm,

or a heaping spoon of peanut butter
should send those hiccups to the gutter.

If your hiccups aren't cured by any of these,
then come back when you need to get rid of a sneeze.

Alliterative Abecedarian

Audacious Abigail Applewhite always argues articulately with antiquarian abecedarians.
Bubbly Bubbie Burgermeister bravely bamboozles burly barbarians.
Charming Chester Chedderworth cheerfully chitchats with chubby chickens.
Daring Darius Dogbreath dutifully delivers dirty diapers.
Eagle-eyed Eddie Ellsworth easily edits erudite editions.
Fortuitous Freddy Ferguson frequently forgets formidable facts.
Garrulous Gwendolyn Gobbledygook giggles good-heartedly at gonzo goggles.
Handsome Horatio Habersham handles hazardous horses heroically.
Illustrious Isabella Ivy industriously identifies irritable idiosyncrasies.
Lamentably lazy Lily Lingerfelt largely lollygags lackadaisically.
Kind-hearted Kennedy Kupchak kickstarts cumbersome kayaks.
Madam Maggie Malarkey magnanimously mollycoddles magnificent manatees.
Neighborly Natasha Niedermeyer knowingly negotiates with gnarly nitwits.

Poems for and about Children

Old-fashioned Oliver Oliphant organizes olive orchards oligarchically.
Pleasant Periwinkle Papadopolus purposefully picks particular purple peaches.
Querulous Quention Quacksalver quills quintessential questions into querying quilts.
Ravenous Rebecca Riddle randomly writes rhyming restaurant reviews.
Secretive Serafina Scarborough surreptitiously skedaddles from scurrilous scalawag's skullduggery.
Terrible Timothy Timberlake teasingly tickles toads on their tummies.
Valiant Victoria Vickers vigorously varnishes velodromes for venerable Venezuelan veterinarians.
Wishy-washy Wally Wainwright wondrously wanders the woods and ways of Willingham.
Xenial Xavier Xanadu excitedly examines exotic x-rays.
Youthful Yolando Youngblood yearnfully yodels, yips, and yawps over yonder every year.
Zany Zachary Zimmerman ziplines with zeal.

Worlds Enough

School Time

Time to get up.
Time to get dressed.
Time to eat.
The most important time of the day.
You've got time.
Time to brush your teeth.
Time to catch the bus.
Do you have the time?
Can't you tell time?
Time for the bell.
Time to take your seat.
Time to do your work.
Test Time.
Take your time.
Not like last time.
I ran out of time.
I hope I do better this time
Just one time I'd like to make a hundred.
Time's up.
Can I have just a little more time?
No time for that.
Time to change classes.
Snack time.
Lunch time.
It's not your time yet.
Play time.
Now is not the time for that.
How I wish it were naptime.
Maybe another time.
There's never enough time.

Is it time yet?
Time to go home.
Study time.
Time for chores.
Dinner time.
Bathtime.
Bedtime.
Time to do it all again.

On Botany and Eminem
for Joey

They say that nothing rhymes with orange,
but if you listen to Eminem
then door hinge meets the minimum
for sounding like orange
way better than storage
or porridge or four inch
and while none of these are exact,
it still remains a fact
that there's a part of a fern
that suits our yearn
to rhyme all the time,
and any botanist will tell you
if you want to remain true
to the desire to rhyme with orange,
there's nothing better to do
than to learn about a sporange.

Dear Humpty Dumpty

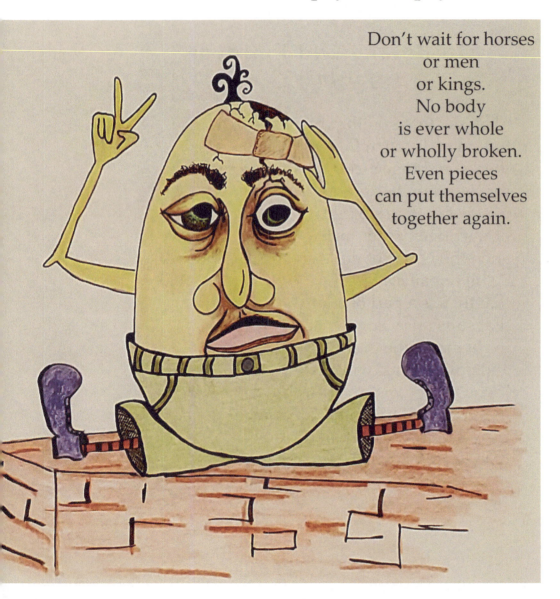

Don't wait for horses
or men
or kings.
No body
is ever whole
or wholly broken.
Even pieces
can put themselves
together again.

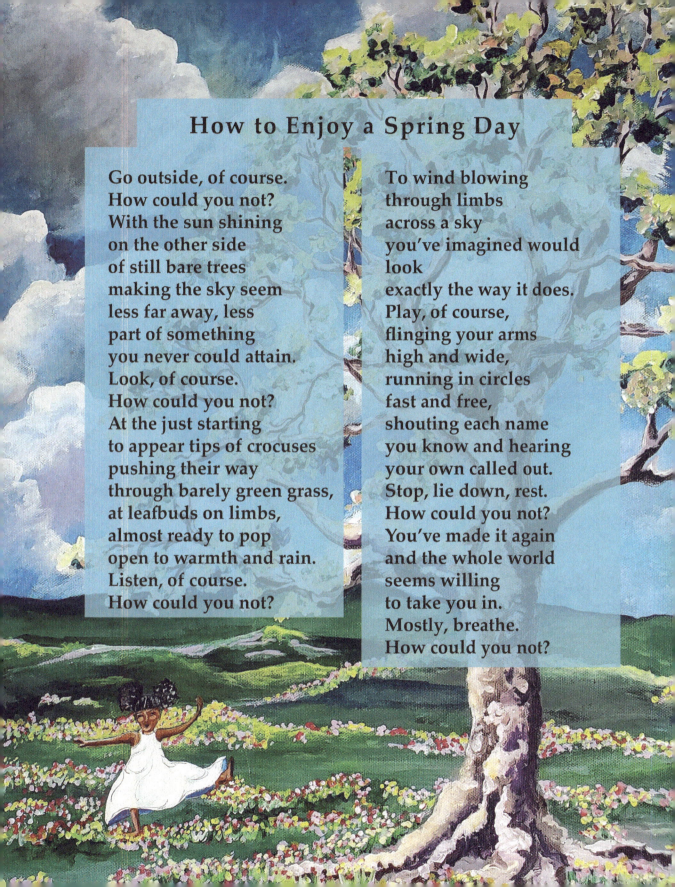

How to Enjoy a Spring Day

Go outside, of course.
How could you not?
With the sun shining
on the other side
of still bare trees
making the sky seem
less far away, less
part of something
you never could attain.
Look, of course.
How could you not?
At the just starting
to appear tips of crocuses
pushing their way
through barely green grass,
at leafbuds on limbs,
almost ready to pop
open to warmth and rain.
Listen, of course.
How could you not?
To wind blowing
through limbs
across a sky
you've imagined would
look
exactly the way it does.
Play, of course,
flinging your arms
high and wide,
running in circles
fast and free,
shouting each name
you know and hearing
your own called out.
Stop, lie down, rest.
How could you not?
You've made it again
and the whole world
seems willing
to take you in.
Mostly, breathe.
How could you not?

Night Travel
after Van Gogh's *Café Terrace at Night*

From here you can imagine
where the painter stood,
just out of sight of self,
looking in from out of darkness.
He captured blues and blacks
surrounding golden light,
circles and rectangles
disappearing beyond sight,
white islands of tables,
barely there shapes of houses,
people holding hands against the dark,
transforming it into something
to be seen, into something
almost beautiful.

Venturing out at night is always like this,
everything wrapped in darkness,
everything wrapped in mystery,
except the warm light waiting at the end.

I'm Thankful for the Week after Next

I'm thankful for tomorrow,
my favorite day of the week,
for the week after next,
and next year, and all the times
that haven't been yet,
for dreams and imagination,
for magic, and wonder, and awe,
for pigs that fly, and fish
with hands, and purple dogs,
and flowers that smell you back,
for what ifs and if onlys
and make believe, and of course
for I think I cans,
for all the places I've yet to see,
all the things I've yet to be,
and all the realms of possibility.

RIDDLE ME THIS

Circles

Circles in circles in circles
pink and peach and periwinkle
brilliant bubbles in the air
blooming with color everywhere
lollipops of every flavor
lovely smells I want to savor
I could sit and watch for hours
a perfect field filled with . . . .

Flowers

Poems for and about Children

Ben's Friend

I can fly in the sky, but I am not a bird.
You can call my name with a 4-letter word.
I don't have to flap since I don't have wings,
and I'm not a balloon but I still need string.
I don't have feathers but I do have a tail.
I might remind you of a rectangle or a sail.
To make me fly start running real fast,
and as long as there's wind, my flying will last.
Give me more string and I'll climb to a great height,
and if you know how to rhyme you'll know I'm a . . . .

Kite

A Bit of Nothing

You see me best in light of day.
In darkness I disappear.
No matter how fast you run away
you know I'll always be near.
Whatever you do
I'll do it too,
the perfect imitator.
I start on one side
then move to the other
and lengthen as the day gets later.
Though some find me scary
you needn't be wary,
for I'll never make a sound.
If you look at the sun
I'll be the one
behind you on the ground.

Your Shadow

I Bet I Can Make You Cry

I won't have to punch you
or call you a name.
I won't take your toys
or make you ashamed.

I won't have to tease you
or make you all sad.
I won't try to scare you
or make you get mad.

In fact, I won't do anything
to make your tears begin.
They'll start on their own
if you cut my skin.

An Onion

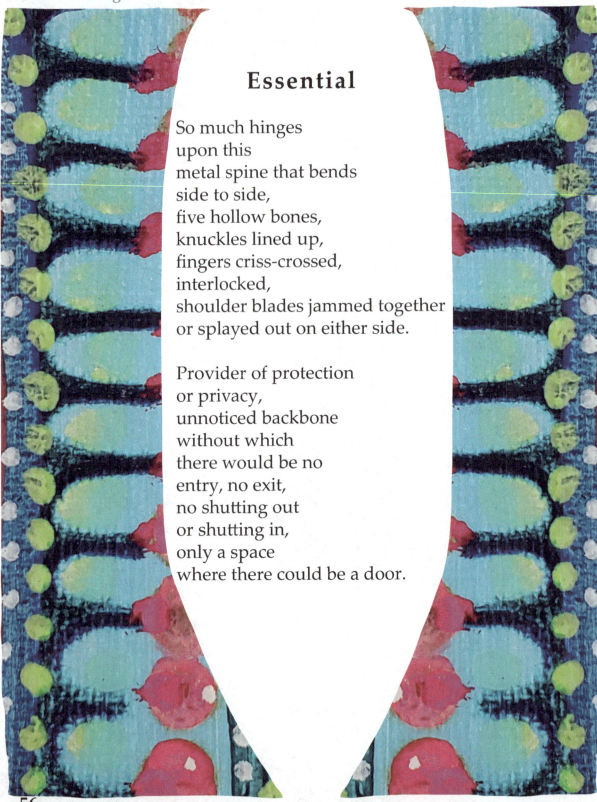

Essential

So much hinges
upon this
metal spine that bends
side to side,
five hollow bones,
knuckles lined up,
fingers criss-crossed,
interlocked,
shoulder blades jammed together
or splayed out on either side.

Provider of protection
or privacy,
unnoticed backbone
without which
there would be no
entry, no exit,
no shutting out
or shutting in,
only a space
where there could be a door.

A Most Unusual Room

No windows, no door.
No ceiling, no floor.
A most unusual room.
Eating it can be your doom.

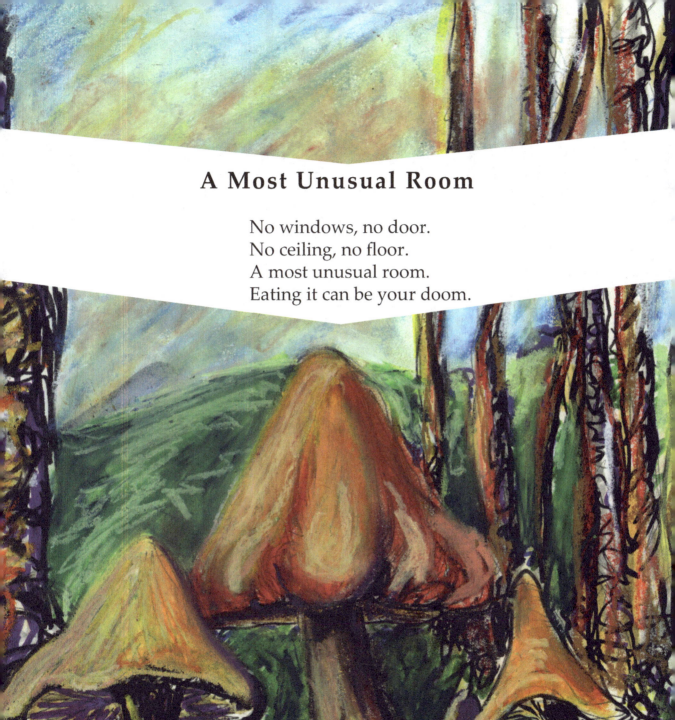

A Mushroom

How To Use U's

Umbrella, Uvula, Umbilical cord,
Umpire, Upholstery, Unbearably bored,
Upstairs, Udder, Uzbekistan,
Utah, Ukelele, Unbelievably grand.
U begins hundred of words we use,
and we always find U's right after Q's,
but no matter how much thinking I do,
I can't find a word that ends with a U.
Side by side two U's make a W.
I know that letter ends quite a few.
But who knows a word that ends in U?
I don't; do you?

Worlds Enough

Besties

There is an I
in this *we*
and a you too
in *you and me*.
You make me happy
when I feel sad,
and I laugh at your jokes
even if they're bad.
When I need to cry
you give me a shoulder,
and when you feel afraid
I make you bolder.
When I want to play
you're always there,
and you know I'll keep
any secret you share.
I always listen
if you need to grumble,
and you pick me up
when I take a tumble.
Any time one of us
is feeling down,
the other finds a way
to get rid of that frown.
Better together
we look out for each other,
strongly connected
like a sister or a brother.
When we're with each other
the fun never ends
because we are always
the best of _____.

spuǝı.ɹℲ

Storm Warning

There was quite a storm at school today
when we were supposed to go out to play.
Dark clouds piled up and chased the sun away,
so we looked out the windows to see what was astray.
Then the wind blew in and sent papers flying,
and howling through the door it sounded like crying.
Then lightning clashed, and flashed, and dashed
and frightening thunder roared like a dinosaur.
It came up so fast it caught us all by surprise.
Some children got scared and started to cry.
And you won't believe what the teacher did.
She went to her desk, crawled under, and hid.
But though the ruckus lasted a while,
no one got hurt, not one single child.
No one even got wet despite buckets of rain
because this storm happened just in my brain
at least until the storm became this poem.

A Brainstorm

Clapperer

Almost empty but full of sound,
shaped like a cup,
but rarely turned up,
much more often heard than seen,
I'm willing to sound off about anything.
I hang from a cow
but I'm not an udder,
and I hang on a ship
but I'm not a rudder.
Usually round but not always
I'm often found in grade school hallways.

Sometimes I'm shiny and made out of brass.
Sometimes I'm used at the end of a class.
Sometimes I ding
and sometimes I dong.
Sometimes I'm short
and sometimes I'm long.
Sometimes I live by a door or a gate,
my favorite place to tintinnabulate.
Wherever I am I'll make it clear
that someone or sometime is getting near.
If you're not sure yet I bet you could tell
from the sound of my knell
that I must be a _____.

A Bell

A FEW HAIKU

By the Numbers

Five syllables to
start the poem, then seven next.
Five again to close.

Poems for and about Children

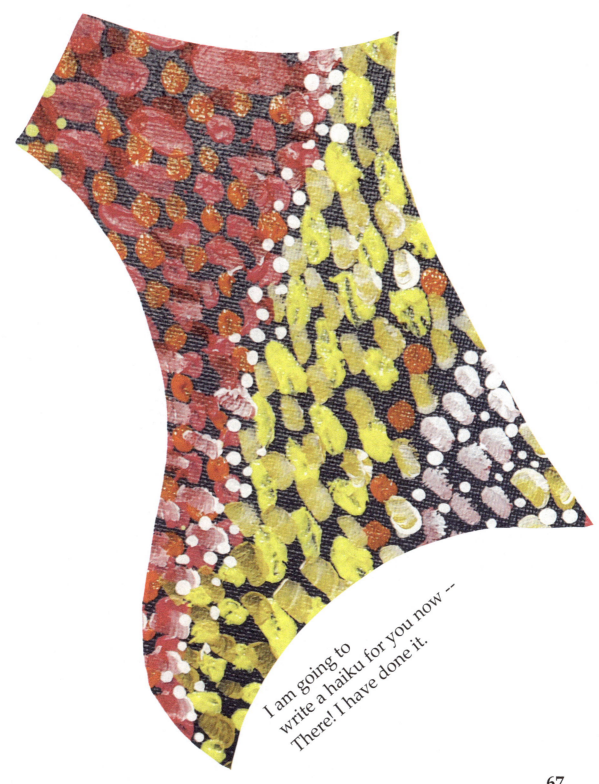

I am going to
write a haiku for you now --
There! I have done it.

Worlds Enough

fashion's
free thinker
the wind wears shirts inside out
and upside down

Poems for and about Children

knee high grass
the dog becomes
a kangaroo

to plant a rose bush
take care – even the smallest
have thorns so beware

Poems for and about Children

backyard lightning bugs –
what it must be like to live
among the stars

Poems for and about Children

honeysuckle smell --
my daughter comes in
from eating summer

Worlds Enough

imagine –
what stories
the silence could tell

WORLDS ENOUGH UNFOLDING

Sky of Endless Stars

Early October morning,
we go for a walk,
you on my back,
and each time we come out
from under the trees
you proclaim the same
3 stars as if they were new,
these 3, worlds enough
unfolding to keep you
in a constant state of wonder.

Sawyer Says

Sawyer asks, *Who was first?*
Where were we all hatched?
Were we babies in God's belly?

Sawyer says we don't need to tell her
what to do, that her mind tells her
what to do. We explain that it's our job
as Mommy and Daddy. She replies,
You need a different job.

When I ask Sawyer what she wants to be,
she says, *A tennis player, a doctor,*
a goose, and an astronaut. She asks if I
want to be an astronaut. I tell her I did
when I was little but now I'm too big.
She says, *You can still be an astronaut.*
You just have to do homework even when you're big.

Sawyer's favorite number is zero.
Do you know how much fun I'm having,
she asks her Uncle Richard who refuses
to let her run up the almost vertical hill
alone. *Zero fun.* And hours later,
coloring, self-contained, as he sits
reading the paper, she reminds him,
I'm still having zero fun.

Eating her Laffy Taffy after days
with a cold, Sawyer says, *I'm cured.*
Now I know why I was sick,
because I wasn't eating enough candy.

Poems for and about Children

Sawyer says, *Aren't you glad I chose you, Daddy? When I was in Mommy's tummy, I saw you and you looked sweet, and I knew you'd be a good Daddy, so I chose you.*

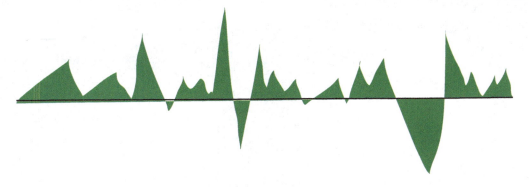

I Teach My Daughter the Joy of Sound

Philomena, she says from the back seat,
a name she's heard but not understood.
I play the game we've played before,
Filibuster? I ask. *No, Philomena*, she says again.

Do you mean *Filibustered Mustard*? I ask,
and hearing her laugh, I know.
Filibustered Mustard who only eats custard?
And the laugh comes again, and I know.

*Filibustered Mustard who only eats custard
and always gets flustered*? and again the laugh,
and then the hand on my arm, and I know in a way
that only such moments make clear, I'm in the right place.

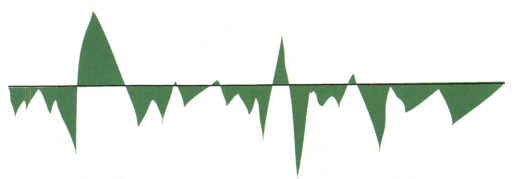

Here Lies

Just a bee
and not a very
extraordinary
one at that
and yet my daughter
who found it,
named it,
nursed it,
would have it honored
as she believes
all living things
deserve such honor
in death at least
if not in life,
and so words
are written
and spoken
and inscribed
on the white
paint paddle's
half a cross:
Here Lies
Buzzy
Just a Bee
and Not a Very
Extraordinary
One at That

The Word for What Only 4-Year Olds Can See

Today my daughter made up a word,
effluctress, to explain why I couldn't see
the rainbow bird outside the window.
Effluctress, she says, *are things
that can only be seen by 4-year olds*,
soda trees, people with wings,
trains that turn into trucks and drive away.

Not the first words she has made up,
for sure, but the first to contradict
what the world tells her can't be,
dragons and dinosaurs, blueberry towns,
her grandma sitting beside her.

Sawyer at 7
Discovers the Roundness of the World

Everything is round, she says,
meatballs and mudpies,
spitballs and balloons,
acorns and rocks and seeds.

How could they ever think
the world was flat?
The sun and moon,
apples and oranges and grapes.

The bodies of animals,
faces, ears, mouths,
the shape our hands make
when they hold each other,
everything we see
through the circles of our eyes.

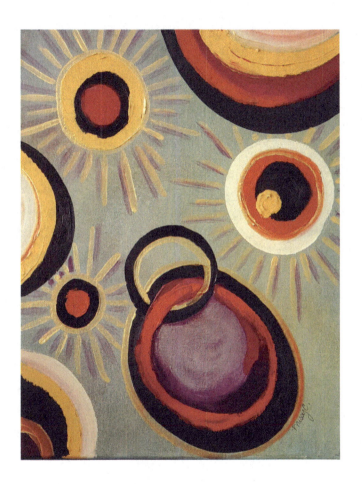

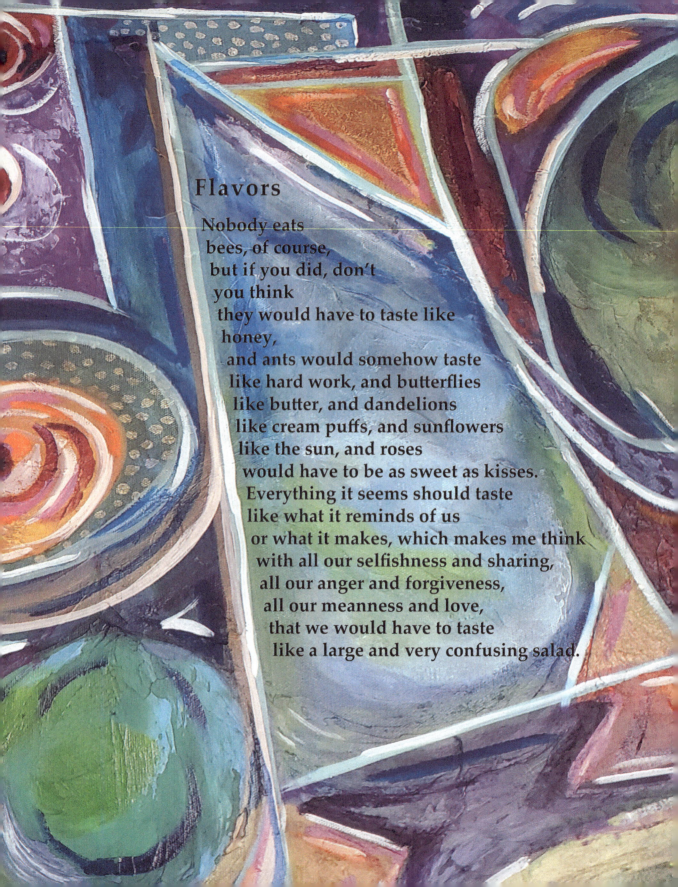

Flavors

Nobody eats
 bees, of course,
  but if you did, don't
   you think
    they would have to taste like
     honey,
      and ants would somehow taste
       like hard work, and butterflies
        like butter, and dandelions
         like cream puffs, and sunflowers
          like the sun, and roses
           would have to be as sweet as kisses.
            Everything it seems should taste
             like what it reminds of us
              or what it makes, which makes me think
               with all our selfishness and sharing,
                all our anger and forgiveness,
                 all our meanness and love,
                  that we would have to taste
                   like a large and very confusing salad.

Headstrong Terry

Headstrong Terry
likes to stand on his head.
He does it almost anywhere,
even in his bed.
He's done it at school
just trying to look cool.
He's done it on a table,
though he wasn't very stable.
He's done it on a mountain
he's just climbed to the top.
He's done it on the sidewalk
in front of a coffee shop.
He's done it on a boat
afloat in the water,
and at a wedding while waiting
for the bride and her father.
He's done it by a lake
on the end of the pier.
He does it anywhere
there's an audience near.
He thinks if he does it
though he's just clowning around,
instead of growing up,
he might grow down.
But it's hard to believe
that it's keeping him young
when just last week
he turned sixty-one.

Words and What They Say

Some say you can't tell anything
from the language that people use,
that Eskimos in fact have no
more words for snow than we,
nor Anglo-Saxons more
for cut, stab, thrust,
and the fact that our words for animals
when we eat them, *beef, pork,*
poultry, all come from French
doesn't prove they're better
cooks or bigger carnivores,
any more than 23 acronyms
for laughter shows that texting
teens just want to have fun,
but when I hear my carful of 2nd graders
from Sandy Ford Montessori School
making up names for the sun,
and the moon, and the stars that only
come out when you're camping and the fire
goes out, and you turn off your flashlights
while your mother holds you in her arms,
I can't help but believe
that not only is there hope for us all
but that the hope we have
is strongest when we find a way
to put it into words.

Of

Poetry is contrary to productivity.
Poetry encourages idleness.
Poetry stands at the window
because it is curious about the flowers,
this flower with its yellow fringed face
around its one brown eye.
Poetry stands at the window
because it is curious about the trees,
this tree with heart-shaped leaves,
some turning yellow in the first
days of fall, some fallen off and still
the limbs reaching up to the sky.
Poetry stands at the window
because it is curious about the sky,
how it got there, where it goes,
what it's like where it ends.
Poetry wants the window down.
Poetry walks back and forth
through a field going nowhere.
Poetry thinks it's okay to look
at the same sky day after day,
sometimes minutes at a time,
sometimes with no other purpose
but remembering blue.

Poetry refuses to follow the rules
of efficiency: *get in line,*
speak only when spoken to,
never say anything that would embarrass your mother.

The first poem ever written was a drum.
The first poem ever written was a foot
tapping on the side of the crib.
The first poem ever written was a rope
slapping the red clay playground
of William Blake Elementary School.

It is not necessary for poetry
to be beautiful
though sometimes it is.
It is not required of poetry
that it be profound
though it rarely closes its eyes.
It is not expected that the face
of poetry be etched with tears,
the hair dripping with sweat,
the mouth expressing awe.
Poetry owes nothing to anyone.

Still, poetry wakes up each morning,
walks to the edge of the world
and jumps, believing one time
it will fly, believing one time
the dive will not end, believing one time
an answer will rise from somewhere beyond.

Assurances

It's lunchtime
and my daughter
home because of the virus
picks basil for her own bruschetta.
I know she's no Greta Thornburg,
and I would never ask her to be,
but she's not texting or tweeting
or googling where to find basil
in one ounce plastic packages
picked from someone else's
commercial garden halfway
around the world.
She knows where to find it
and how to cut the branch
above the lowest pair of leaves
and what to do with it
once she has it.
It's only basil you may say,
and no, she may never save
the world, but how many other
15 year olds know where and how,
and will take the time to harvest
and prepare on their own,
and I think it shows at the very least
that something her mother and I
have taught her has stuck
and it likely will again
some unfathomable number
of years from now
when someone we've yet to meet
calls her, Mother.

Onomatopoeia 101

Flipflop,
Drip, drop,
Tick, tock, boom!

Clap, zap,
pitter patter,
clatter, chirp, and chatter.

Snicker-snack,
click and clack,
wham, slam, bam!

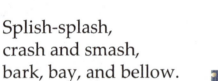

Splish-splash,
crash and smash,
bark, bay, and bellow.

Hoot and howl,
giggle and growl,
mutter, flutter, and pow!

Murmur and whirr,
peep and purr,
gurgle, gargle, and grunt.

Shush and hush,
rustle and bustle,
snap, crackle, and pop!

Babbling brooks and buzzing bees,
cuckoo clocks and chickadees,
whooping cranes and whippoorwills.

Crunch and roar,
squish and rap,
and shoes that go tippity-tap.

Instruments that twang,
bells that go clang,
fires that sizzle and spit.

Whisper and mumble,
hiss and bumble,
rattle, creak and moan.

Boing and boink,
thump and thud,
and sometimes just kerplunk.

Honk and beep,
whizz and vroom
in things that go zip and zoom.

Clamor and crack,
scrabble and scratch,
splat, whack, and quack.

Whimper and screech,
snort and slurp,
hiccup, belch, and burp.

Worlds Enough

Plop, plop, fizz, fizz,
tinkle and crinkle
squeak, squeal, squawk, and squall.
Fine examples, one and all
of
On
O
Mat
O
P-O-E-I-A
A word that means words
that mean what they say.

About the Author

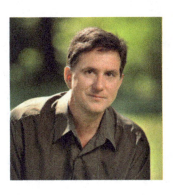

Scott Owens holds degrees from Ohio University, UNC Charlotte, and UNC Greensboro. He is Professor of Poetry at Lenoir Rhyne University, former editor of *Wild Goose Poetry Review* and *Southern Poetry Review*. He owns and operates Taste Full Beans Coffeehouse and Gallery and coordinates Poetry Hickory. He is the author of 17 collections of poetry and recipient of awards from the Academy of American Poets, the Pushcart Prize Anthology, the Next Generation/Indie Lit Awards, the North Carolina Writers Network, the North Carolina Poetry Society, and the Poetry Society of South Carolina. He has been featured on The Writer's Almanac seven times, and his articles about poetry have been featured frequently in *Poet's Market*.

About the Artist

Missy Cleveland attended East Carolina University, Greenville, N.C. with studies in fashion merchandising and marketing. She is a self-taught artist with thirty years as a muralist and decorative painter. She was a co-founder of "Bottega" an artist boutique in Hickory, N.C. Currently Missy is producing custom commission canvases for the public and for Old Hickory Tannery, a Newton, N.C. based furniture company. "World's Enough" is her first published book of illustrations. She was able to, in part, through a grant awarded from the United Arts Council of Catawba County and invaluable collaborations with Redhawk publishing.

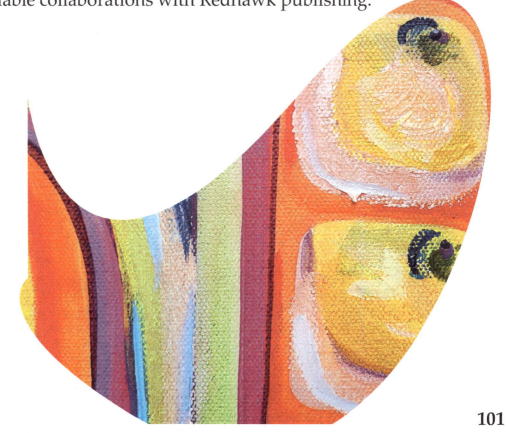

Made in the USA
Columbia, SC
05 June 2022